D0984581

Masters of Music

ILLUSTRATED BY PAUL NEWLAND

SCHUBERT

Masters of Music

SCHUBERT

Percy M. Young

Ernest Benn Limited · London
David White · New York

FIRST PUBLISHED 1970

BY ERNEST BENN LIMITED

BOUVERIE HOUSE, FLEET STREET

LONDON, EC4

&

DAVID WHITE

60 EAST 55TH STREET, NEW YORK, NY10022

© PERCY M. YOUNG 1970

ILLUSTRATIONS © ERNEST BENN LIMITED 1970

PRINTED IN GREAT BRITAIN

ISBN 0   510–13732–6

LIBRARY OF CONGRESS CATALOG CARD NUMBER

U.S.A. 87250–240–6 *(Trade)*

87250–438–7 *(Library)*

Contents

Illustrations

Preface

THE FACT THAT so much of the music of Schubert is among the greatest ever written, that it is—as we often say— immortal, raises many questions. What was the nature of Schubert's genius? To what extent was his music affected by environment? What is the relationship between our pleasure in this music and Schubert's lifetime of rebellion, poverty, and ill-health?

Schubert's songs, and some of his instrumental works, are as near perfection in music as seems possible. Because for a long time this has been accepted as being the case, the life and personality of the composer have frequently been idealised. He has been shown as an amiable young man of unworldly temperament, sustained by kind friends in a community of great cultural awareness, who had the misfortune to die young. The truth is rather different.

Schubert was amiable, but sometimes he used his friends. He was not as unworldly as is made out; it was just that he did not like the world as he saw it. His reputed liking for horse-play and his drinking habits were not in themselves entirely admirable; but today, perhaps, we can understand them as reactions to frustration. In modern terms Schubert would be described by some as a drop-out, and deplored because he "protested". Others would see him as a genius, with a supreme gift for registering his criticism of society and his hopes for a better world in song. There is something here for us to think about, for in some respects Schubert anticipated the feelings of many young people of today.

9

The musical society of Vienna, generally praised for its culture, had no great cause for satisfaction over the case of Franz Schubert. There were honourable exceptions, but very few of those who prided themselves on their love of music cared whether he lived or died. With proper care, indeed, he would not have died.

If Schubert had lived in a better, more humane, society he would have been a different person. Possibly he would have gone on being a schoolteacher. But his music would have been very different. We can compare his life with that of his brother Ferdinand, who did accept the conditions of life as they were. He too was a composer; but not a great composer. In the eyes of his community, however, Ferdinand was successful, whereas Franz was a failure. We know otherwise. But sometimes we should consider how great art comes painfully into being. We may then appreciate the more the artist's vision.

P.M.Y.

1. *A Vienna Schoolmaster*

VIENNA WAS A FINE PLACE at the end of the eighteenth century. It was the capital of a great Empire—which was still called the Holy Roman Empire until 1804—and the cultural centre of Europe. Maria Theresa and Joseph II by a combination of courage and cunning had managed to keep the far-flung imperial possessions together; they had built fine new buildings in and about Vienna; and they had governed their subjects with some degree of tolerance. They had encouraged the arts, and, helped by an aristocracy with time, money, and sometimes taste, at its disposal, had made Vienna for ever famous for its music.

Mozart, Haydn, Beethoven, all had strong associations with the city. To us, looking down the long corridor of time, it seems as if Vienna in those days was a veritable fairyland. Whether it appeared so in, say, 1780 depended on who you were.

Vienna—central Vienna that is—was peopled by court officials, by a nobility drawn from every part of central Europe, by their retainers, and by tradesmen, craftsmen, and others, who ministered to the needs of those who could afford to have their needs ministered to. From far away places in Bohemia, Hungary, Poland, and so on, subjects of the Empire, otherwise compelled to make a poor living on the land, came into Vienna hoping to find its streets paved with gold.

Franz Theodor Schubert, whose ancestors had been Moravian peasants, was among them. Franz Theodor, however, could have had few illusions. His ambition was to be a schoolmaster, which was not among the most highly re-warded occupations. He aimed to qualify himself by first serving an apprenticeship to his brother Karl, who kept a school somewhere near the Augarten (a famous pleasure garden). In 1785 Franz Theodor married a young woman named Elisabeth Vietz, a native of Silesia, who had been a domestic servant until her marriage. She was seven years older than her husband, who was appointed schoolmaster in the suburb of Himmelpfortgrund soon after their marriage.

Here, to the north-west of the city centre, there was little of the splendour of the capital. This was a labouring com-munity. The houses were small, and inadequate to the needs of the large families who inhabited them. Children spilled out into the squalid courtyards and the narrow streets along which the waggons passed to and from Döbling, Heiligen-stadt, and Grinzing. But, as often where conditions are least favourable, there was a good deal of cheerfulness about. Viennese humour (not always in the best taste) was rife, and ran in and out of the folk-songs which were frequent entertainment. Itinerant harpists and fiddlers came that way to add more flavour to the music of the people. Beyond the village (as it was) were gardens and meadows, and vine-yards, and the hills of the Vienna Woods, of Kahlenberg and Leopoldsberg.

In 1796 Franz Theodor Schubert moved into a house on the road to Nussdorf and it was here on January 31, 1797, that Franz Peter Schubert was born. There had previously been born to the Schuberts eleven children, of whom three boys survived infancy: Ignaz (b. 1785), Ferdinand (b. 1794), and Karl (b. 1795). Of the six daughters of the household,

Franz Peter Schubert

one, Maria Theresa, who was four years younger than Franz Peter, survived.

Those were difficult times for the parents of large families, and were not made easier when the French invaded Austria in 1797. On October 17 Austria made peace, and concessions. The Empire was beginning to fray at the edges. French ambitions grew and as other great powers sought to contain them Napoleon became more determined than ever to dominate Europe. In 1805 the French invaded Austria again; Napoleon installed himself in the Palace of Schönbrunn near Vienna; the Viennese were forced to support occupation troops and in January 1806 an inglorious treaty was signed at Pressburg, which brought only temporary respite. In 1809 Napoleon again declared war on Austria, and once again the Austrians were defeated.

These were the years in which Haydn and Beethoven composed great works in Vienna and for the Viennese. They were the years in which Franz Schubert grew into boyhood. It was intended from the start that he should in due course follow his father's profession; simply because it was easier that way. The hereditary principle worked throughout society. Franz learned to play the violin and the piano at home, and when he was nine or so he was passed on to Michael Holzer, organist of Lichtenthal Parish Church, the church in which Franz had been christened and in which the family regularly worshipped. A Baroque building, completed in 1729 and rebuilt forty years later, this church possessed a fine High Altar designed by one of the Schönbrunn Palace architects, Hohenberg von Hetzendorf. The effect of such works of art on impressionable boys like Franz Schubert may not be exactly estimated, but it was considerable. Michael Holzer was a fine musician, but he had his limitations. He was seventy years old, and it was well-known that he had a tendency to drink too much too often. Franz Schubert was a problem for him. The old man was kind and did his best to give instruction in singing, organ, harmony, piano, and violin; but he soon felt that he could not keep up with such a bright pupil as Schubert proved to be.

On September 30, 1808, Schubert was auditioned by Antonio Salieri (1750–1825), the Court Music Director, for a place in the court choir. Having been accepted he became a pupil in the *Stadtkonvikt*—the boarding-school at which the choristers were then educated. This institution was housed in the buildings which had belonged to the old university, formerly directed by the Jesuits but taken from their control by Joseph II in accordance with his programme of liberalisation. The *Konvikt*, although draughty and uncomfortable, had an atmosphere of its own. Schubert, although only a mile or two from his own home, as a court chorister found himself in an entirely different world.

The Parish Church at Lichtenthal

2. Chorister in the Royal Chapel

ON SUNDAYS and on the major Church Festivals Schubert sang in the court chapel, one of the palace buildings about the Schweizer Hof. Dressed in a dark-brown uniform, with gold epaulette on the left shoulder, white cravat, knee-breeches with buckles, shoes with buckles, and three-cornered hat, he sang the works of the Haydns, and Mozart, of older church composers, and of modern masters. One of these was Salieri himself. Another was Peter von Winter (1755–1825), a court composer at Munich whose chief claim to fame is that Mozart disliked him. Winter's church music, at its worst excessively sentimental, was, however, much esteemed in Vienna. But Schubert did not think much of it. In a copy of Winter's First Mass once used in the court chapel there is a note by Schubert: "Croaked out for the last time, 26 July, 1812".

Life in the *Konvikt* was tough. Boys were required to work hard and were given little in the way of holiday. They were not even allowed to go home every year during the main autumn break. Food was always in short supply, as Schubert observed in one of his letters to his brother Ferdinand, in which he also asked for help with money. But there were compensations. There were many opportunities to learn about music in the best possible way; through practical experience. Josef Kenner, who was fellow-pupil and later wrote poems which Schubert set to music, told how Schubert,

Albert Stadler, already a composer, and Anton Holzapfel, used to go off into a music-room, in the free time after the midday meal, to play and sing pieces by Beethoven and Johann Zumsteeg (1760–1802). Zumsteeg, a friend of Friedrich Schiller (1748–1812), and court musician at Stuttgart, was an important song composer, and his music appealed strongly to boys of Schubert's generation.

Joseph von Spaun, a university student some eight years older than Schubert, according to the instruction of the Director of the *Konvikt* had formed a students' orchestra there. Very soon he noticed that Franz Schubert was a good violinist, and before long he promoted him to lead the first violins. Schubert was thrilled by this opportunity of getting to know the masterpieces of music that were then modern at first hand. He was specially moved by the expressive slow movements of Haydn's symphonies, by the G minor Symphony of Mozart (K.550), and by the Second, Fifth, and Seventh Symphonies of Beethoven. He thought the overture to *The Marriage of Figaro* the finest ever written, was greatly interested in the overtures of Etienne Méhul (1763–1817); but an overture by the fashionable Abbé Georg Vogler (1749–1814), which pleased everyone in Vienna, did not appeal to him at all.

The *Konvikt* orchestra was conducted by the old court organist Ruczicka, who was not always regular in attendance. When he was absent Schubert took his place. It was Ruczicka who, having tried to teach Schubert to play from "figured bass" (a bass line only with figures which indicate the harmonies to the player), said like Holzer before long that there was nothing more he could teach the boy.

Living conditions in the *Konvikt* were hardly ideal, for the educational system in general was antiquated; but in one

B

The Stadtkonvikt

respect the authorities were more enlightened than would have been the case in most places at that time. A boy with a gift for music was neither thought a freak, nor discouraged. In fact the reverse was the case. When he was thirteen Schubert composed a Fantasia for piano duet. A year later his setting of a poem (by a poet named Schücking) *Hagar's Lament*, which had also been set by Zumsteeg, caused Salieri to pay special attention to his pupil's creative talents, which, even in a musical community, seemed remarkable. Schubert wrote other songs—including his first settings of poems by Schiller—and four overtures for the school orchestra.

In 1811 Schubert was taken to see his first opera. This was *The Swiss Family*, a lively piece by Josef Haydn's godson Josef Weigl (1766–1846), which had been composed two years earlier. It is interesting that this piece, the first ever to be translated into Czech, was an inspiration for the earliest Czech operas. It was also an inspiration for Schubert, whose determination to compose music for the theatre was further sharpened when, in 1813, he saw Gluck's *Iphigenia in Tauris*. The principal singers in this production were Anna Milder (1785–1838), and Michael Vogl (1768–1840), both of whom later became famous through their association with Schubert. On the same occasion Schubert met the poet and dramatist Theodor Körner (1791–1813).

During 1813 Schubert wrote numerous songs, a number of dances, a Symphony in D major, a cantata for his father's name-day (see p. 24), and other works. At the end of the year, his time at the *Konvikt* being up, he had to decide what to do. He knew what he was expected to do; he saw no way of evading what appeared as his duty. He enrolled in a training school for teachers, which was near St Anna's Church in the city.

Meanwhile conditions at home had changed, for in the summer of 1812 Schubert's mother had died. A year later his father remarried, his new wife being Anna Kleyenböck. Later on she was to show a commendable interest in Franz's career—to the extent of helping him by loans from out of the housekeeping money.

While he was supposed to be learning the techniques of school-teaching Schubert continued zealously to compose, and among his compositions were string quartets in D and B flat major (Op. 168) (in the first place to be played at home) and a Mass in F major. The B flat Quartet is an eager, impulsive, work, marked by Schubert's characteristic probing of distant tonal relationships, by dramatic interjections which were part and parcel of the mood of the times, and by a fine appreciation of string sonorities. The Mass, however, appeared as more of a landmark at the time.

Composed in honour of the centenary of the foundation of the parish church in Lichtenthal this work was duly performed on October 16, 1814. Old Holzer graciously allowed Schubert to conduct the performance. Ferdinand Schubert played the organ, and Therese Grob, daughter of a deceased local silk manufacturer, sang the solo soprano part. The parishioners of Lichtenthal, having heard the Mass, agreed that schoolmaster Schubert's son was a genius. Salieri, who was present, did not dissent from this opinion and arranged a second performance of the work in St Augustine's Church. The Mass, from the point of view of the people of Lichtenthal, was not too high-brow. Most of it sounded as they thought music in church should sound. It bore a strong resemblance to well-loved works by Winter. The "Kyrie" of Schubert's Mass begins in this way:

Ky - ri-e   e - lei-son, e - lei-son. Ky - ri-e

Between the two performances of his Mass Schubert, who had been reading Goethe's *Faust,* composed one of his most famous songs, *Gretchen at the Spinning Wheel*—the words being taken from *Faust.*

3. *Friends and Patrons*

AFTER THE END of the Napoleonic Wars the statesmen of
Europe came together in Vienna in 1814 and 1815 to try to
find a way to prevent such calamities happening again. Unfortunately they were more often concerned with national
self-interest than the common good, so that the results of
their deliberations left much to be desired.

While they were in Vienna for the Congress the leaders
of the nations—and the many diplomats and assistants who
accompanied them—had no cause for complaint at the way
in which they were treated. The Emperor Franz I spent
£800,000 on entertaining his distinguished guests—while
his demobilised soldiers walked the streets hoping that one
day they might be paid, and while his secret police kept
watch for signs of internal disorder. Visitors were unaware
that the Austrian soldiers had not been paid, and either did
not know of or were indifferent to the activities of the police.
In general they found Vienna a gay, lively city where dan-
cing went on night after night. The popular dance of Vienna
was the waltz. Through the Congress of Vienna it became
popular all over Europe and North America.

Schubert was a child of his age, and like other Romantic
artists and philosophers he aimed at opening people's minds
to the beauty of the world. The greatest of the Romantics—
Schubert among them—made this their aim because they
saw too much that was ugly and evil in the human situation.
Nature did better than man, which is why nature was so im-

portant to the poet, the painter, the musician. So far as its buildings and its surroundings were concerned, Vienna in Schubert's day was generally said to be—beautiful. But the disparity between wealth and poverty, the way in which the aristocrats held on to privilege, and the frequent support given by leaders of the Church to reactionary ideas and to intolerance, represented ugliness. To Schubert and his friends the society that looked so fine from without was rotten at the core. How he loathed symbols of corruption and injustice—like the castle built for a mistress by a corrupt priest (see p. 62), but what could he do as a schoolmaster? He needed more freedom to express his point of view—which was also the point of view of a generation.

For a little while Schubert helped in his father's school, and in 1816 he tried to obtain a post in a new school of music just established by the Philharmonic Society of Laibach (now Ljubljana, in Yugoslavia). Armed with a recommendation from Salieri (who, however, gave testimonials to three other candidates) Schubert made a serious attempt to succeed in his application. He played the organ, and the violin, he said, and was well able to teach singing as well. He added that in his opinion he was the best candidate for the job. The canons of the cathedral and the committee were not of the same opinion, and appointed Franz Sokol (1779–1822), whose sole claim to fame is that he succeeded where Schubert failed.

Meanwhile Schubert was increasing his circle of friends. Joseph von Spaun introduced him first to the poetry of Johann Mayrhofer (1787–1836) and then to Mayrhofer himself. Mayrhofer lived in rooms that had previously been occupied by Theodor Körner, and Schubert became a frequent visitor. He had another reason for visiting the house, since the landlady was the mother of an old school friend at the *Konvikt*. He found that the poet expressed many of his own views both on social and philosophical questions. These were sometimes idealistic, sometimes cynical, often pessimistic, and occasionally optimistic. At that time poetry was the art that was most fertile in ideas; it was also an art in which ideas could be expressed in such a manner that they did not catch the sharp eye of the censor.

Another companion of this period was Franz von Schober, a wealthy amateur who came to Vienna to study law, but, having found Schubert, almost entirely devoted himself to looking after his friend's talents. Schober was also a poet, and the author of some of the most famous of the texts of Schubert's songs, including that of *To Music*.

Joseph von Spaun and a friend, Josef Witteczek, had rooms in the house of Heinrich Watteroth, a history teacher whose free-thinking and unorthodoxy put him on the wrong side of the Church but very much on the right side of his pupils. Watteroth was yet another of those immediately won over by Schubert's personality and obvious genius.

During these years Schubert—out of work—lived a hand-to-mouth existence, staying with his friends and being generously supported by them. Watteroth was kind enough to disguise his charity by commissioning a cantata for his "name-day". (In a Catholic country a person celebrates the festival of the Saint after whom he is named.) He paid the composer 100 gulden for the score of a cantata which was subsequently lost.

In the summer of 1818 Schubert was introduced to the Esterházys—the noble, fabulously wealthy, Hungarian family which had employed Haydn—and was offered a holiday job. He was to teach the children of Count Johann

Franz von Schober and Johann Mayrhofer

Esterházy at his country home (one of several) at Zselesz, in
Hungary. At first Schubert enjoyed the country, which he
described in detail to his brothers and his friends, but without friends he soon found himself bored. Lodged in the
servants' quarters, and obliged to eat his meals in the servants' hall, he longed to be back in Vienna. While at Zselesz
he had obligingly found time to help out his brother Ferdinand. Now well up the educational ladder, and a teacher at
the Imperial Orphanage in Vienna, Ferdinand needed a
"German Requiem" for the children of his school with those
of the so-called "Normal High School" to sing. Franz did

25

his best to emulate the old German manner, as this chorale-
like music for the Gospel shows.

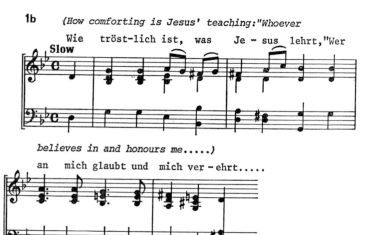

Ferdinand thought that this sounded so much like his own
style (he was a composer too) that in the autumn of 1818, at
the first performance, he announced it as his own. Franz
was surprised, and more surprised when in 1826 this Mass
was published by Diabelli as Ferdinand Schubert's Op. 2.

When he returned to Vienna Franz settled in to live with
Mayrhofer, and proceeded to establish himself in the esteem
of those who really appreciated music. These were not only
those who liked music, but those to whom music was an important means of understanding the purpose of life. Already
in the winter of 1818–19 his music was becoming tolerably
well-known in Vienna. His songs were frequently performed
at private parties: his *Prometheus* Cantata (written for
Watteroth) was given a hearing at the expense of Ignaz

Sonnleithner, father of one of Schubert's friends, and an important figure in Viennese musical life; on February 28, 1819, a well-known tenor, Franz Jäger, gave a performance of the *Shepherd's Lament* (a setting of a poem by Goethe) which aroused favourable notice in the press; and on March 14 an overture was played by an amateur music society.

Schubert was twenty-two years of age, a failed schoolteacher, foot-loose in a city where indolence was not unfamiliar, and where ambitions easily dissolved in the free-and-easy life of the coffee-house and the tavern. And yet he had already achieved more than many composers accomplish in a lifetime; he had composed some of the best-loved music ever written.

On April 17, 1817, Joseph von Spaun took it on himself to write a letter to the great Goethe, sending with it a set of Schubert's settings of Goethe's poems. He spoke of Schubert's talent, of his friends' wish to see his works published. Schubert, von Spaun insisted, was a master, and especially a master of "German" song. Not only had he set poems by Goethe, but also by Schiller, Friedrich Klopstock (1724–1803), Friedrich von Matthisson (1761–1831), Ludwig Hölty (1748–76), and other famous poets. Goethe—he was then sixty-eight years old—returned the manuscript without comment.

The truth was that Goethe's musical judgement was much influenced by the Berlin choral director, teacher, and Bach expert, Carl Friedrich Zelter (1738–1832). Zelter had set Goethe's lyrics to music, and so had such other respected composers as Johann Friedrich Reichardt (1752–1814) and Zumsteeg. These were composers of Goethe's generation, brought up in a tradition which he understood. Of Schubert he knew nothing, nor did he seem to wish to know anything.

4. *Words and Music*

IT IS OFTEN SUGGESTED that Schubert "created" German song—which in this case is always called by the German word for song—*Lied*. This is not true. The history of *Lied* was already a long one when Schubert arrived to make his own unique contribution to it.

Serious consideration of the musical setting of the German language arose during the time of Martin Luther. During the two hundred years that followed the Reformation many literary societies, both aristocratic and middle-class, were established in which the relationship between poetry and music was a perpetual topic for conversation. In the first part of the eighteenth century poets and musicians in Germany found that they had much in common. In both arts the frequent aim was to "imitate" (or to describe) nature— and this came to include human nature. Further, the great development in the classical age of German literature caused musicians, when they could, to emphasise German qualities in a musical sense.

Carl Philipp Emanuel Bach (1714–88) was friendly with the leaders of literary thought in Leipzig, Berlin, and Hamburg, and in his vocal music showed himself aware of the manner in which the meaning of words could be intensified not only by melody but also harmony and figures of piano accompaniment. His half-brother Johann Christoph Friedrich Bach (1732–95) was a close friend of Johann Gottfried von Herder (1744–1803), whose poems and libretti he frequently set to music. J. C. F. Bach was a frequent contributor to a weekly musical journal edited by C. P. E. Bach

Schubert, Mayrhofer, and Schober at Freyung

and he published settings of poems by, among others, Klopstock, Hölty, and Matthias Claudius (1740–1815). These
were also some of the poets whose lyrics provided inspiration
for Schubert. They were among the pioneers of Romantic
thought, bringing into poetry a new vision of the influence
of nature and a fresh understanding of human personality.
Schubert not only set their poems to music, but also conveyed
the spirit of the poets through his music.

In the first place the composers who preceded Schubert
aimed at satisfying the market. Songs were popular for

music-making among middle-class amateurs. They preferred, therefore, the easy strophic form (the same melody
for each verse), which was also convenient for the publishers
of the weekly magazines in which many such songs first
appeared. But for the concert-room, or the court salon, the
dramatic cantata was cultivated. A famous cantata text was
Ramler's *Ino*, set to music both by Telemann and J. C. F.
Bach. Whatever the song, however, composers set out to write
expressively. An example of landscape illustration is shown
here in the opening bars of a song by Friedrich Wilhelm Rust
(1739–96), one of those who pointed the direction which
Schubert was to follow. We feel the soft evening breeze in
the movement in the left hand of the accompaniment.

This is from a setting of a poem by a poet much favoured
by Schubert—Friedrich Matthisson—and was published in
1796. Reichardt's *Restless Love* was written about the same
time, and published in a collection of Goethe songs in 1809.
Here we notice the dramatic quality of the writing—in

3a

With lively movement

the backing up of voice by piano—and the way in which this conveys a restlessness of the spirit. In such a song, we may say that man and nature are at one, which is what was strongly believed at the time when Schubert was growing into manhood. It is interesting to compare Schubert's setting of *Restless Love* (1815) with Reichardt's. Without being told, it would be difficult to decide which was by Reichardt and which by Schubert. How Schubert handles the same passage is shown on the next page.

Schubert was fully aware of what had taken place in the field of German song, and his closest friends were poets, or writers, or philosophers. Musically Schubert was supremely gifted. He did not, however, have the one most useful talent, of being able to harness his genius to some steady appoint-

3b

ment. Had he been organist, or Kapellmeister, or had he succeeded in his application at Laibach, he would have had to control his creative gifts for some practical purpose. He would also have been obliged to subordinate his opinions, even in respect of music to those of his employers. But he opted out of the system and being free from direction by those who held the reins of power was able to practise the art of self-expression more than most. He gave up "security" of course, and condemned himself to poverty. But life had it compensations. Austria in those days was not what we would describe as a "free society". The police kept a strict control on political views, and the dignitaries of the Church did their best to ensure that orthodox opinions were maintained. As a composer Schubert had his own means of expressing what he felt and thought, and so he discovered his own sort of freedom.

Between 1811 and 1828 Schubert composed approximately six hundred songs. Of these more than half were written in three years, in 1815, 1816, and 1817. In the early period the influence of Goethe was very strong, and both *The Erl King* and *Hedge Rose*—two of the most popular of Schubert's settings of Goethe—like *Restless Love* were composed in 1815. These two songs are widely contrasted; the first is a dramatic ballad, the second a song of almost folk-song-like simplicity. But, just as Schubert was quick to seize on any poem put before him, so was he quick to see what kind of music was required to convey the atmosphere or the significance of a particular poem.

The Erl King also attracted Reichardt, who made an effective setting of the poem twenty years earlier than Schubert. *Death and the Maiden* and *The Trout* are among the most familiar of Schubert's songs, and both belonged to 1817. The words of the first were by Matthias Claudius. Those of the second were by one of Claudius' contemporaries, Christian Schubart (1739–91), who was not only a gifted lyrical poet but also a trenchant critic of autocratic rulers. Schubart was a Romantic writer. Schubert was a Romantic musician. It is worth remembering that for those who believed in it as a liberating force Romanticism implied concern not only for nature but also for people. This concern is surely to be felt in the music of *Death and the Maiden* and *The Trout*. The melodies of these songs became even more familiar because they were used as themes for variations, the one in the Piano Quintet in A major (Op. 114), and the other in the String Quartet in D minor (no. 14) of 1824. There is no composer of modern times whose music is so deeply rooted in song as Schubert. There is no composer of

c

4

any time who had laid such a foundation in song as had Schubert by the time he was twenty years old.

It will be recognised in the twentieth century that song is one medium by which youth may show its dissatisfaction on the one hand and its ideals on the other. Schubert belonged to a group which had small regard for the customary conventions or for the advice or opinions of the old. The songs that Schubert composed had a passion that had not previously been at all common, and they had a purpose.

Schubert was aware of the loneliness of disillusionment. He expressed it at the end of the song *Solitude* (1818) in this way.

Then as now men longed for peace. Schubert wrote this longing into the last bars of *Faith in Spring*, composed in 1820.

5

as introduction to song.

5. *Poets and Painters*

DURING HIS BOYHOOD Schubert had tried his hand at most forms of music. His chamber music was played at his father's house and among his friends. His orchestral music, if performed at all, was played by the *Konvikt* orchestra, or by other amateurs. Of the early orchestral works the *Overture in Italian Style* in C major (1817) is interesting because it showed Schubert enjoying himself in light-hearted parody at the expense of Rossini, who was at the time extremely popular in Vienna. The Fourth Symphony, in C minor, Schubert described as "The Tragic" and it shows the composer trying to live up to the dramatic implications of the subtitle, but hardly succeeding. In 1816, the year in which this was composed, the light-hearted Fifth Symphony in B flat major also appeared. These are works which in their lyrical deportment and easy flow seem to bypass Beethoven and to come straight from the sunnier ways of the Mozart–Haydn tradition.

In the summer of 1819 Schubert went with Vogl to Steyr, a small and delightful town in Upper Styria about mid-way between Vienna and Salzburg. Vogl had been born there and through him Schubert met a number of people during the three months of his visit. He stayed in Steyr in the house of a Dr Schellmann, in whose daughters and also in the daughters of Schellmann's neighbour Schubert took a great deal of flirtatious interest. In Linz, 20 miles to the north, Schubert and Vogl paid a call on von Spaun's mother. What was most gratifying, however, was that Sylvester Paumgartner, of

'*Atzenbruggerfest*'

Steyr, should commission the "Trout" Quintet (Op. 114)
for piano and strings, which was duly performed in Paumgartner's house during the winter. The last movement is a
set of variations on the theme of the song.

For the next year or two Schubert enjoyed a summer
holiday in the country. In July, 1820, together with Schober,
he went to Atzenbrugg. In the following year the two friends
went there again, and then for a month to St Pölten some
way out of Vienna to the west.

The July days of 1821, in Atzenbrugg, were, so to speak,
set to music. A collection of German dances (from which

Schumann and Brahms learned a thing or two) were composed, and a great delight they are.

In Vienna Schubert lived what might be termed a regular irregular life. In the mornings he composed. In the afternoons he sometimes worked, but more often walked in the parklands of the distant suburb of Währing. Evenings were often exhausted in inns and coffee-houses, but sometimes they were devoted to performances of Schubert's music.

The company he kept was lively, rebellious, creative, and often infuriating. One evening in 1820 Schubert and some friends were at the rooms of Johann Senn, a former student of the *Konvikt*. Senn was known to the police, for he belonged to a revolutionary student movement, and while Schubert and his friends were there the police called, demanding to examine Senn's papers. The young men made it clear to the police what they thought of them, and they were taken into custody. All were released with an admonition, except Senn, who was expelled from Vienna.

Adam and Eve charade at a 'Schubertiad',
from a painting by Kupelwieser

Schubert had no difficulty in making friends, and among
them were Moritz von Schwind (1804–71) and Leopold
Kupelwieser (1796–1862), artists who left many recollec tions
of the Schubert circle in their paintings and drawings.
Friendship with these two artists may seem to have a special
significance, since—to a considerable extent—it can be seen
that they and Schubert often pursued similar aims. Kupelwieser and von Schwind were exponents of "Biedermeier"
art—a kind of art that flourished in Austria and Germany
between about 1815 and 1848. In this the artist concerned

39

himself with small-scale works suitable for the middle class which now provided patronage for the artist. The drawings, aquarelles, and book illustrations of these painters were the visual counterpart to the song with piano accompaniment.

The most important of the Viennese Biedermeier painters was Ferdinand Waldmüller (1793–1865), who once painted Beethoven's portrait. Waldmüller's landscapes, at once realistic and idealistic, and filled with light, have effects of colour that may be perceived, perhaps, in changed form in Schubert's songs. Kupelwieser was a minor master of the Vienna Biedermeier school, and its characteristics are evident in his pictures of Schubertian society; in, for example, an aquarelle describing an Adam and Eve charade at a "Schubertiad", or in a country sketch showing Schubert and his companions at Atzenbrugg. Moritz von Schwind was a more versatile artist with a lively imagination and a neat hand. He was a medium whereby German legend—of knights and princesses, and fairy glades—came into the imagination of many people through finely worked drawings. There is a kind of musicality about von Schwind's work—whether in the lines of his drawings or the harmonies of his landscapes—which is not altogether surprising. He loved music. In 1825 he made a series of thirty illustrations for *The Marriage of Figaro*. Forty years later he decorated the loggia of the State Opera in Vienna with motivs from *The Magic Flute*.

Perhaps no musician was as lucky as Schubert in the quality of his friends. Through von Spaun he met Spaun's cousin, the poet and dramatist Matthäus von Collin. Through Sonnleithner he met the sisters Fröhlich—four lively and musical girls who seemed to know everyone—and through them the dramatist Franz Grillparzer. Through von Schwind he met Eduard Bauernfeld, who was to become famous as

*A country party at Atzenbrugg, from a
painting by Kupelwieser*

the translator of the works of Shakespeare and Dickens. In
1821 his friends, taking Schubert's affairs out of his hands,
began the publication of some of his songs. By the end of the
year twenty were available in print. They were eagerly
bought up, and not only by his friends. To some of the
songs he had added Dedications, in respect of which some of
the dedicatees were pleased to pay a free-will offering to the
composer. At that time it was not uncommon to dedicate
music, or literature, to a person of distinction with the hope
that he might make some friendly and useful response.
". . . I must tell you," Schubert wrote to von Spaun, "my
dedications have done their work; that is to say [Ladislaus
Pyrker] has forked out 12 ducats, and . . . [Moritz von]
Fries 20, which is a very good thing for me".

6. *Unfinished Works*

SCHUBERT WAS GRATEFULLY SURPRISED when his music brought him money, but he was not so indifferent to worldly matters as to think that he should not try to furnish himself with an income. The difficulty was, either that he did not fit into any convenient category, or that he was unfortunate in his business dealings. This was particularly the case in respect of the theatre. Schubert always hoped that he would meet with success in the field of opera, and even before he was twenty he had composed as many as eight operettas. Some of these were at the instigation of friends like Stadler, Mayrhofer, and Körner, who, perhaps, were also even at this time beginning to claim a little corner of immortality on Schubert's account. None of these pieces were in any way important and none were performed in his lifetime. Afterwards occasional performances were given as acts of homage.

In Schubert's day there were five important theatres in Vienna, the two court theatres—*Am Kärntner Tor* (the *Kärntnertor* theatre) and *In der Burg* (the Burg theatre) — and the suburban theatres, *In der Leopoldstadt, In der Josefstadt,* and *An der Wien.* These five theatres, with varied traditions and appealing to different sections of the community, offered many possibilities to a composer. But a good libretto was needed for an opera, or a good play for incidental music, if he was to achieve any kind of success.

In 1819, when he was living with Mayrhofer, Schubert set to work on a one-act opera, *Die Zwillingsbrüder* (The Twin

Brothers), at the suggestion of Vogl, who promised that he could arrange a performance at the *Kärntnertor* theatre. The libretto by G. E. von Hofmann, who wrote and translated libretti for a living, was bad. The operetta ran for a week and was taken off. At the end of the first performance there was a call for the composer—from his friends. Because he was not dressed for the occasion Schubert refused to take a curtain call, and Vogl apologised to the audience, telling them that the composer was not present.

Despite this failure Schubert was commissioned by the management of the theatre *An der Wien* to provide incidental music for a melodrama by Hofmann, *Die Zauberharfe* (The Magic Harp). This was written to show off the effectiveness of the mechanical devices of the theatre and it was largely pantomime. Schubert wrote the music in a fortnight, not caring much whether it succeeded or failed. It failed. The play lasted for a week, at the end of which the management defaulted and he never received his fee.

In 1821 Schubert was commissioned to write an aria and a duet to add to Ferdinand Hérold's (1791–1833) *La Clochette*, for production at the *Kärntnertor*. Unfortunately his additions were considered too serious for this four-year-old lightweight opera (a great box-office draw all over Europe), so that was but one more disappointment. In the same year Schubert set to work on Schober's *Alfonso and Estrella*, on which he set high hopes. The first stages of this work belong to the gay summer of 1821, when Schubert and his friends stayed first at Atzenbrugg and then at St Pölten. Schober had relatives in both places who were able to offer hospitality.

Schubert continued work on *Alfonso and Estrella* when he returned to Vienna, and was most interested to meet Carl Maria von Weber (1786–1826) when he came to Vienna to conduct the first Viennese performance of his new opera, *Der Freischütz*, at the *Kärntnertor* on November 3. This was the most successful German opera ever composed up to this point, and in Germany it has remained one of the most popular and, in many ways, the most typical. Schubert dearly wanted to succeed as an opera composer, but he was always defeated by his libretti. *Alfonso and Estrella*—the favourite among his operas—is hampered by a trite, melodramatic, plot that was a non-starter even in Schubert's day. There is, however, some beautiful descriptive music in this extensive score, and the songs are distinguished by an Italian grace. Both qualities may be heard together in the greeting to spring at the end of the first Act. The voices of country-people are heard in the distance, accompanied by harp and woodwind (placed off-stage):

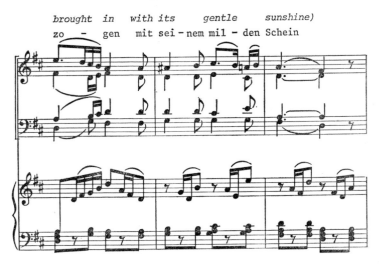

brought in with its gentle sunshine)
zo — gen mit sei — nem mil — den Schein

Alfonso and Estrella was not staged until years after Schubert's death; nor was *Fierrabras*, a three-act opera to a libretto by Joseph Kupelwieser, the brother of Leopold. The story came from a twelfth-century French epic, which had been turned into a German novel in the sixteenth century. In composing music for such romantic stories (*Fierrabras*, alas, was very tedious in Kupelwieser's version) Schubert learned to control large orchestral forces. For the sake of colour he allowed himself more instruments than in his earlier symphonies. In this way he further extended his means of depicting emotion. The beginning of the *Fierrabras* overture shows the "terror and mystery" atmosphere which was so much exploited by poets, novelists, and musicians, during the Romantic period.

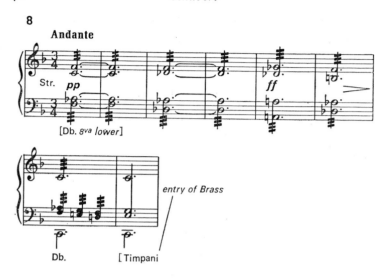

Schubert attempted other works for the stage, but only one deserves notice. That is the play *Rosamunde*, by Helmina von Chézy (1783–1856), who also wrote the libretto for Weber's opera *Euryanthe*. Schubert heard the first performance of *Euryanthe* in Vienna on October 25, 1823, and told Weber that he thought it much less good than *Der Freischütz*. Nevertheless he did not diagnose that the reason for the rather cool reception of this work was an inefficient libretto: or if he did, he reckoned that that for *Rosamunde* could not be equally poor. It was, and the play for which Schubert composed some nine numbers was taken off after two performances at the theatre *An der Wien*. The music was put away and forgotten for more than forty years (see p. 77).

During the period in which he was making his unsuccessful assault on the theatre Schubert was engaged in many

Wilhelm Müller

other enterprises. In 1821 he hopefully left Mayrhofer's apartment and hired rooms of his own in the Wipplinger-strasse. He managed to pay the rent for twelve months, after which he gave up the attempt to maintain his own quarters and moved in with Schober.

In the spring of 1821 Schubert set more poems by Goethe and the two following years were productive so far as songs were concerned. Apart from the classical poets Schubert drew on the lyrics written by his friends, including

Mayrhofer, von Collin, and Schober. In 1823 he composed *Auf dem Wasser zu singen* (To be sung on the water), the poem being by Friedrich von Stolberg; a number of settings of poems by Friedrich Rückert (1788–1866), including the beautiful *Du bist die Ruh*; (Thou art peace) and the song cycle *Die schöne Müllerin* (The beautiful maid of the mill).

The author of this famous set of poems was Wilhelm Müller (1794–1827). Müller's poetry corresponded in some part to the work of the Biedermeier artists (see p. 39), and the title-pages of the early edition of the Schubert–Müller songs carry typical Biedermeier-like illustrations. Müller was a nature-lover, with an enthusiasm for travel, and a greater enthusiasm for wine. He had the talent to write down his impressions in neat, often sentimental, verses that were gratefully received by the German middle class.

Schubert made the poems much more significant by his musical commentary. There is a good deal of truth in the suggestion from his friend Franz Grillparzer (1791–1872) that in music (with words) "the commentary is better than the text, the understatement as audible as the statement. . . ." This is certainly true of Schubert's settings of Müller.

At that time, and for a long time afterwards, the Viennese prided themselves on the musical quality of the "atmosphere" of the city. This was rationalised by Grillparzer, who extended music to include the music of speech, of thought, and of feeling. That Mozart and Haydn had lately lived in the city, and that Beethoven and Schubert were living there, was sufficient to impress on writers like Mayrhofer and Grillparzer (as well as others) the force of the argument. They felt in particular that Schubert more than any other composer expressed the musicality of the atmosphere. This atmosphere pervades every part of Schubert's music. It is to be felt in works which now are accepted as important as well as in those which are not, but which once gave considerable pleasure. The part-song for male voice's *Die Nacht* (The Night), of 1822, is no masterpiece, but it does convey a "Viennese" atmosphere in its easy lilt, in the shifting nature of the harmonies, and in its sentimentality. This conveys the idea of Schubert at his most easy-going.

In April, 1822, a set of Schubert's variations on a French theme, for piano duet, was published. This was dedicated to Beethoven and it is said that Schubert took a copy to present to that master in person, but did not find him at home. Beethoven afterwards used to play this work with some pleasure with his nephew Carl. By now Schubert was managing to place a number of his piano works with publishers and his waltzes and other dances became increasingly popular. The

D

Illustration from the second edition of Die Schöne
Müllerin

most important work for piano, however, was the Fantasia,
known as "The Wanderer" because the *adagio* second
movement is built on a theme from the song of that title, of
1816. The "Wanderer" Fantasia (Op. 15) is remarkable
among Schubert's piano works for its demands on the
pianist, and also for its compact organisation. The foundation of the work is this rhythmic pattern.

The "Wanderer" Fantasia suggests that Schubert had
been studying the dramatic characteristics of Beethoven.
There are two works, one before and one after the Fantasia, which have a special place among his works and which

have an intensity of passion, a concentration of emotion, which also belong to the spiritual world of Beethoven. They are the "Quartet movement" of 1820, and the two symphonic movements of 1822. The last-named constitute the "Unfinished Symphony".

When Schubert had been a pupil of Salieri he had got to know Anselm Hüttenbrenner, who in due course left Vienna to live near Graz. Schubert was able to maintain contact with him because Anselm's brother Josef became so attached to him that he gave up most of his own interests to devote himself to those of the young composer. Josef Hüttenbrenner acted as secretary, aide, and promoter. It was he who, in 1822, tried to interest theatres in Munich and Prague as well as in Vienna in a new operatic venture of Schubert, and the Leipzig publishing house of Peters in his songs. In 1822 Schubert was elected as honorary member of the Styrian Musical Society at Graz. From 1823 until 1865 Anselm Hüttenbrenner, who was closely associated with this Society, had the manuscript of what we now know as the "Unfinished Symphony".

It is supposed that Schubert wrote this work—despatched by Josef Hüttenbrenner to his brother—as a mark of appreciation of the honour done to him by the musicians at Graz. Regarding its being unfinished the question is, and will remain, an open one. Maybe Schubert, who left sketches at least for the scherzo, never got round to completing it. He had done this before (anyway, it is not all that unusual for people not always to finish what they set out to do!) and would do it again. In all Schubert left unfinished more than twenty works of which this symphony, the movement for string quartet, and the C major piano sonata, of 1825, are the most important. Perhaps Anselm Hüttenbrenner lost

some of the work, which was why he did not tell anybody
about it until 1865. Though in this connection it must be
said that after Schubert's death many people lost interest in
him, and many of his manuscripts lay undisturbed for years.

But the "Unfinished" had a particular fascination because
it was unfinished, and on this account furnished many additions to the romantic lore of music and musicians. The two
extant movements take their place in the repertoire simply
because they have a quality, the quality described as Schubertian, not to be found in other symphonies. In the first movement the distance, in emotional terms, between the first and
second main themes might appear to be unbridgeable. The
first theme may be said to be dark and ominous; the second
is gay and light. The measure of Schubert's skill in thematic
organisation is, perhaps, best appreciated in the last 57 bars
of the first movement in which the two principal ideas are
shown not so much as opposites as two complementary
parts of one whole. The slow movement shows Schubert's
unpredictable imagination, in search of a contentment he
hoped might exist but which he was never to find. The end
of this movement is as a serene landscape, with gentle lights
playing over it.

10

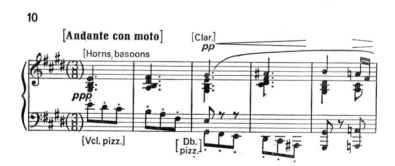

7. Two Worlds

THE "UNFINISHED" SYMPHONY may be felt to symbolise darkness and light, fear and hope, war and peace. This kind of symbolisation is written into the very nature of symphonic form, into its structure of contrasts of key and motiv. But the more we move into the nineteenth century the more we find that symphony seems to relate to personality. This, basically, is what Romanticism was about.

At the time at which he was thinking of and, indeed, composing the "Unfinished" Symphony Schubert was ill. He contracted venereal disease, which was particularly rife in Vienna at that time. He left Schober's quarters and went to live with his father and step-mother. Since 1817 Franz Theodor Schubert had been in charge of a school in the suburb of Rossau, and it was here that Franz Peter stayed from the end of 1822 until the May following when he was so ill that he had to be admitted to the General Hospital in Vienna as an in-patient. His health, weakened not only by this particular disease but also by his general habits in the course of the next few years, was to go from bad to worse. There were some cheerful interludes to relieve what otherwise was a life of discontent, disorder, squalor, and sheer misery.

The story of the artist at odds with society is one which many people have written. It is not one, however, which only belongs to the past. At the present day, especially in some Western countries, there are many young people in revolt who live very much after the Romantic manner. Schubert

would be regarded by the conventional as a "drop-out".
So in one sense he was. But, despairing of one world he
built another. The beauty of his music (see Ex. 10, p. 52)
stands out sharply against the dark background of his life.
He was, perhaps, the most typical Romantic among composers.

Early in 1823, as always badly in need of money, Schubert
sold his rights in a considerable number of his works to the
publishing firm of Diabelli. He let them go (as have other
composers) for a lot less than they proved to be worth. In
April he placed some of his songs with another publisher,
but his financial prospects showed no improvement. The
year passed miserably, except for a brief summer holiday in
Styria where he was happy to see von Spaun, Mayrhofer, and
Vogl. In the following year Schubert's circle of friendship
underwent a change. The old familiarity with Schober and
Mayrhofer diminished; Vogl was no longer so ready to sing
Schubert's songs at informal gatherings; and Kupelwieser
went to study in Italy. Bauernfeld, however, was on more
intimate terms, and von Schwind, full of compassion for the
man and admiration for the artist, was a constant companion.
On March 31, 1824, Schubert wrote to Kupelwieser in this
vein:

> . . . Think of a man whose highest hopes have come to
> nought, to whom love and friendship offer nothing but
> pain, whose enthusiasm for what is beautiful . . . threatens
> to vanish. Ask yourself if this is not a miserable, luckless,
> man . . . I would pass my days without joy and without
> friends, were it not for Schwind who sometimes visits me
> and turns on a ray from those sweet days of time past.

In the summer there was again a brighter interlude, for

he was once again invited to the Esterházy estate at Zselesz. As before Schubert was grateful to be in the country, and his pupils—the Count's daughters—had made sufficient progress for him to have written some difficult piano duets for them to play. These included a "grand sonata" (Op. 140), a set of variations (Op. 35), and a *Divertissement à la hongroise*, in which he paid a small tribute to the idiom of the country.

Interest in Hungarian music had been stimulated by the recent publication in Vienna of sets of Hungarian dances arranged by Jozsef Bengraf (1745–91) and Ferdinand Kauer (1751–1831). Kauer was living in Vienna, where he conducted at the Leopoldstadt theatre. Schubert put what he thought was a suitable Hungarian mood into the opening of his *Divertissement*.

11

The decorative notes are useful in suggesting the rhapsodic character of the village music he may well have heard in Hungary.

During 1824, in which his hopes were so low, Schubert wrote some of his finest compositions. The paradox grows, how a man who was so disillusioned, who had so little to hold on to, could as an artist progressively develop in stature.

The String Quartet in A minor (Op. 29), the first version of the "Death and the Maiden" Quartet, and the Octet for clarinet, horn, bassoon, and strings (Op. 166) all belong to this year. The Quartet was given its first performance in March by the quartet led by Ignaz Schuppanzigh (1776–1830), the principal violinist in Vienna. In gratitude Schubert dedicated this Quartet to him. The Octet was commissioned by a clarinet-playing nobleman, Count Ferdinand Troyer, and the theme on which the variations movement is based was taken from an ill-fated Mayrhofer–Schubert opera, *Die Freunde von Salamanka* (one of those mentioned on p. 42). In that year the first part of *Die schöne Müllerin* was published. The dedication of these songs was to Count Carl von Schönstein, who had not only consistently supported Schubert's claims to greatness but, being a fine baritone singer, had done a great deal to make his songs known.

On February 14 Moritz von Schwind wrote to Schober:

Schubert is in good health, and after a standstill period is once again busy. He has recently come to live in the neighbouring house—where the inn is; in a nice room on the second floor. We see one another daily and so far as I can I share all his life.

Schubert's friendship with Moritz von Schwind became very intimate at this time and the two were almost inseparable. At the same time his friendship with Bauernfeld also grew more intense. A few months earlier Schubert had complained that he was alone and friendless. Now he no longer felt that he was alone and deserted. As the spring of 1825 approached his fortunes, like his health, seemed to be on the mend.

Anna Milder (1785–1838), the singer for whom Beethoven wrote the part of Leonore in *Fidelio*, sang Schubert's songs in Berlin. Sophie Müller, another famous Viennese singer, gave the first performance in March of his recently written *Die junge Nonne* (The Young Nun), and entertained both him and Vogl at her home near Schönbrunn. Favourable notices of Schubert's songs appeared in Berlin and Dresden, and he began to publish with the firm of Artaria. The Philharmonic Society promoted concerts at which Schubert's songs and vocal quartets were performed.

In April the Piano Sonata in A minor (Op. 42) was written and Schubert began his settings of the poems from Walter Scott's *The Lady of the Lake* which he hoped would make his name known in England. To this end the English words, as well as the German translation, were printed. In June the publication of some of Schubert's settings of Goethe and the dedication of one of them to him prompted him to write to the poet. Once more, however, there was no response from Weimar, where Goethe lived. It was not until 1830, when a famous German singer sang *The Erl King* to Goethe that he really took note of the rare and remarkable quality of Schubert's music. By then, so far as Schubert was concerned, it was too late.

8. *Growing Reputation*

AT THE END OF MAY, 1825, Schubert left Vienna with Vogl and travelled to the west, to Upper Austria. Here he stayed until the beginning of October. This period of four months was one of the happiest of Schubert's life. Not only did he find his spirit renewed by the enchantment of the country, but he met a surprising number of people to whom neither his name nor his compositions were unfamiliar.

Until the beginning of June Schubert stayed in Steyr, where he had enjoyed himself six years earlier. He was the guest of Countess Weiszenwolf, an admirer of his music. He then went with Vogl to Gmunden, a beautiful holiday centre on the Traun See—one of the lakes in the neighbourhood of Salzburg. During his six weeks here Schubert is said to have worked at a symphony, of which, however, there is now no trace. From Gmunden he followed the river Traun northward to Linz, where he was disappointed not to find von Spaun. He was only moderately compensated for the absence of his friend by the excellence of the local beer. He reported to von Spaun that those who had heard them liked his Walter Scott songs (especially the *Ave Maria*) very much; and having learned that von Spaun was meeting Franz Xaver Wolfgang Mozart (1791–1844), the son of Wolfgang Amadeus, at Lwow in Poland, he sent greetings to him. In Upper Austria Schubert was in Mozart's native country.

From Linz Schubert returned to Steyr, where he wrote home in high spirits. He had visited the monasteries of St Florian and Kremsmünster. These two buildings (or, rather, groups of buildings) were among the finest works of the great Austrian architect Jakob Prandtauer, and they housed men of feeling and sensitivity. The Benedictine house of Kremsmünster supported a famous observatory, and an exclusive school for young noblemen at one time. Schubert was well received by the monks and said how much they appreciated his music. He had played the variations from his A minor Sonata to them and, assisted by a competent partner, various pieces for piano duet.

He went on to write of the breathtaking beauty of the mountains, and the lakes. But these also seemed sometimes to menace human existence, for in comparison man appeared as a very frail creature indeed. Schubert poured his impressions of the scenery into the songs *Die Allmacht* (The Omnipotence) and *Das Heimweh* (Home-sickness), of which the words were by Ladislaus Pyrker.

On September 22 Schubert wrote a long and detailed letter to his brother Ferdinand, about the beauty of the landscape, and of the villages amid the hills; the peasant houses which showed occasional traces of former splendour in marble supports to windows and doors that were now shabby; the city of Salzburg, with its churches and palaces set amid the encircling hills. But Salzburg had fallen on evil days. There were not many people to be seen in the streets; a number of buildings were empty; and grass was growing between the stones in the city squares. Salzburg had suffered not only during the Napoleonic Wars, but from the great fire of 1818.

Schubert found rooms for himself in Salzburg at No 8 Juden Gasse (Lane of the Jews) and explored the city thoroughly. He went to the Cathedral, "a heavy building after the pattern of St Peter's, Rome", and to St Peter's Monastery. Here he found a monument to Josef Haydn, and

Schubert and Vogl at the piano

paused a moment to think about his "peaceful, pure spirit". He also reflected on Michael Haydn, Josef's brother, who had lived most of his life in Salzburg, and was much admired by Ferdinand Schubert.

A week after writing to his brother Schubert sent a letter to Bauernfeld, and on September 21 he wrote another long letter to Ferdinand. Now he was once again at Steyr, and he had more to say about his country excursions. He had visited a castle built by a "spiritual" prince—a bishop, that is, who enjoyed princely privileges— for his girl-friend in a month, without anyone complaining at the expense; he had been into the mountains to a place where not so many years before Bavarians and Italians had fought each other over a few acres of disputed Tyrol territory; he had seen sacred images all over the country, and wondered how many more times the crucifix would be used to bless what he called "deeds of shame". Schubert was deeply religious; but he was, according to the Church's rules, a bad churchman. He was impatient of authority, and unwilling to accept that as things had been so they should remain.

In October Schubert returned to Vienna, where he found Schober and Kupelwieser—both returned from abroad—to greet him, as well as Bauernfeld and Schwind. It was a cheerful time, and parties were frequent and went on late into the night. One publishing house, anxious to capitalise on Schubert's growing reputation, had a print made from a portrait by Wilhelm Rieder. Others readily took his works and published them without much regard to contractual equity. The reviewers in Leipzig and Frankfurt paid tribute to Schubert's genius. But none of this made life secure.

In the spring of 1826 Schubert applied for the post of deputy music director at court, which, had he been success-

The river at Steyr

ful, would also have given him the opportunity of conducting at the *Kärntnertor* theatre. He was, however, unsuccessful in his application. Josef Weigl was preferred, and
even Schubert himself thought that this was a good choice.

In the summer it was pleasant to be able to go out of the
city to Währing, just outside Vienna, where Bauernfeld
lived with his mother. It was at Währing during this summer
that Schubert wrote his incomparable settings of Shakespeare,
and also his String Quartet in G major (Op. 161), which
tests the medium with an enormous range of expression,
and demands great concentration on the part of the listener.
This is a masterpiece of instrumentation; the great gestures
of introduction recollect, perhaps, the massive Alps that a
few months earlier had made such an impression on the composer. The tonal wanderings of the slow movement are filled
with that sense of mystery which he felt in the landscape of
Upper Austria. The poet Shelley was contemporary with
Schubert. What Shelley expressed in one medium so did
Schubert in another. The String Quartet in G major catches
at Shelley's sense of wonder as

> The everlasting universe of things
> Flows through the mind . . .

In October Schubert offered the dedication of one of his
symphonies (which one is not known) to the Philharmonic
Society, and since the Society responded by presenting him
with 100 florins he found it possible once more for a time to
live independently. He moved into pleasant rooms at 7
Bäckerstrasse, not far from his old school.

Autumn passed into winter. Schubert's friends rallied
loyally round him, and performances of his songs were
regularly given at Schober's or von Spaun's. At one of these

gatherings, which was the subject of a famous drawing by von Schwind, Vogl sang some thirty songs. On December 2 the overture to *Alfonso and Estrella* was played at the *Kärntnertor* theatre. This performance was reported in the London music journal *The Harmonicon* (p. 118) in 1827, which referred to "a revived Overture by Schubert, full of striking effects, and well worthy of being better known." Later in that year the same journal (p. 168) carried another notice concerning Schubert from a correspondent in Vienna:

> In our Society of Music [in Vienna] were given two new songs, composed by the favourite Schubert, which excited general interest. The first was *Die zürnende Diana* (The Wrathful Diana), the second, the Forrester's Song, from Sir W. Scott's *Lady of the Lake*.

9. *Winter's Journey*

IN EARLY TIMES the contrast between winter and summer, and the contrast between life and death, provided the essential matter for almost all of art and poetry. In Schubert, perhaps more than in any other musician of his period, one is made aware to what extent these same thoughts were uppermost in the minds of people hardly more than a century and a half ago. The period which is described for convenience as the "Romantic" period was anything but romantic in many of its aspects. The chances of contracting disease, of dying prematurely, were strong in Schubert's Vienna. In spite of its famous buildings, many parts of the city were dirty, squalid, and — being overcrowded — breeding-grounds for every kind of contagion. Edward Holmes, the English writer, visited Vienna in 1827. There were, he said, fine shops, particularly for jewellery and women's clothes, but —

> Most of the passages leading to the ramparts . . . are not very agreeable, especially those leading from the narrower streets, as their detestable stench is continually reminding an Englishman of . . . [his] nose, that discriminates.

The best people left the city in the summer not only because it was pleasant to do so, but because it was necessary; under the hot sun the air was intolerable. So, when he could, Schubert also went away in the summer months.

These conditions sharpened the vision. The perceptive artist, aware of the true power of the summer–winter contrast, put this into his works with feeling. Schubert's *Die schöne Müllerin* cycle shows the composer mainly in idyllic, sunny, mood. In the cycle of songs entitled *Winterreise,* composed in 1827 and of which the poet again was Müller, Schubert captured more sombre moods. The atmosphere is reflected in the general title—Winter's Journey.

Schubert composed the first part of *Winterreise* at the beginning of 1827. At the time he was living near the Karolinentor, but in the autumn he moved to Schober's lodgings. At the time when Schubert was composing his *Winterreise* songs Beethoven was lying on his sick-bed reading through a score of some of Schubert's works that had been given to him. "Truly," he is reported to have said, "in Schubert there is a divine spark." On March 19 Schubert, together with the Hüttenbrenners, went to visit Beethoven, but to his distress found him already almost out of life. A week later Beethoven died, and Schubert was among those who carried torches at his funeral on March 29.

In the summer Schubert and Schober went to Dornbach, which was near enough to Vienna to allow them to return to the city from time to time. In the autumn there was a trip to Graz, at the invitation of a notable hostess of that town, Mrs Marie Pachler. Schubert owed this invitation to a friend, Johann Baptist Jenger, who was well-known in those parts as a member of the Styrian Musical Society and a friend of the Pachlers. Mrs Pachler, wife of a lawyer, was a good pianist, and she had been a friend of Beethoven. She had a great admiration for Schubert and she and her family entertained him with a sympathetic concern for his needs.

When he wanted to play music, a musical evening was arranged. If he wished to talk, then congenial company was invited to meet him; the Styrian poet, Gottfried von Leitner, the lawyer Franz Haring, the musical director of the theatre,

Kinsky, an art dealer named Kienreich, for instance. There were excursions into the country, and in the park at Hallerschlössel there is a memorial tablet to the pleasant hours which Schubert spent there. On one evening Schubert took part in a concert of the Styrian Musical Society. On another he went to the theatre to see a performance of Giacomo Meyerbeer's (1791–1864) *Il Crociato in Egitto*, which he enjoyed.

While in Graz Schubert composed some more dances — the *12 Grätzer Walzer* — and one or two songs. These included his setting of Herder's version of the Scottish ballad *Edward*. He went back to Vienna on September 20 taking with him some of Leitner's poems, which he set and dedicated to Mrs Pachler. Schubert was invited back to Graz for the summer of 1828 by the Pachlers. He was also invited to Gmunden again by Ferdinand Traweger, with whom he had stayed before. But when the time came he could not afford the money for the journey.

Back in Vienna Schubert was miserable. His health was bad, and gave rise to depression. But he wrote the last twelve songs of *Winterreise* to complete the cycle, as well as the two trios — in B flat (Op. 99) and E flat (Op. 100) — for violin, cello, and piano, and the *Impromptus* and *Moments musicals* (*musicaux*) for piano. The songs were thought to be very difficult to understand. In *Die schöne Müllerin* Schubert had followed the strophic principle (with the same melody for each verse). In the second cycle for the most part he did not do this — much to the chagrin of those German critics who thought that German songs should be set in strophic manner. There was also the matter of mood. Schubert's friends were put off by the note of melancholy that sounded throughout the cycle.

The town of Graz

But, like Mozart and Beethoven, Schubert could rise triumphantly over personal difficulties and ill health. In the Trio in B flat he asserted the principle of life—in this way:

12

With Schubert, as later with Brahms and Dvořák, the three-note (triplet) group had a particular vitality and exhilaration. It is to be encountered in two other familiar works of the last year of Schubert's life—the song *The Shepherd on the Rocks* (Op. 129), with piano and clarinet accompaniment, and the great C major Symphony.

In the song Schubert seems to indicate the shapes of the Austrian Alps in the free-ranging arpeggio of the melody, which the triplet seems to keep air-borne.

The clarinet echoes the voice, and this again gives a feeling of space, while, as in the Trio in the same key, changes to remote key centres give a sense of mystery. In the C major Symphony of 1828 triplet figuration gives a special kind of flavour to the second theme of the first movement. By itself this theme shows the influence of Bohemian music, which was much to be heard in Vienna in those days when many of the city's musicians came from the Bohemian part of the Empire.

14

Schubert turned into 1828 not without hope. He had
been elected in the previous year to membership of the
Vienna Philharmonic Society, which, taking into account
the similar honour done to him at Linz and Graz, indicated
that some people in responsible places were taking notice of
his achievement. In January the B flat Trio was played at a

A musical evening at the house of Joseph von Spaun

cheerful party at von Spauns' home—to celebrate von Spaun's engagement. In March some of Schubert's friends arranged a public concert of his music in one of the rooms of the Philharmonic Society building. During this month he finished the C major Symphony. This, one of the greatest masterpieces of symphonic music, was composed for the Philharmonic Society. The orchestral players took one look at the music and said it was too difficult. It was not played during Schubert's lifetime.

73

During this year Schubert was feverishly busy. Percipient musicians unknown to him wrote to praise his music, and publishers in various German cities tried to get him to supply works for their lists. In the summer—when there was no holiday—and autumn, Schubert wrote the last of his songs, published after his death as *Swan Songs*, a string quartet, the last three piano sonatas, as well as some church music. His energy was matched by a mastery of effect, as in the song *Der Doppelgänger*, of design, as in the B flat Sonata. In the first of these works the sinister other self of Heinrich Heine's poem is suggested by:

15a

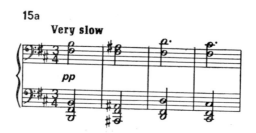

In the second work the point of departure is a marvellously calm statement, of Beethoven quality:

15b

Schubert was ill again, and his brother Ferdinand took him into his home. On November 3 he went, with difficulty, to the parish church of the suburb of Hernals to hear a Requiem Mass composed by Ferdinand. It was the last music he heard. The following day he went to Simon Sechter (1788–1867), the court organist, for a lesson in counterpoint. Feeling that he was not as good in this craft as he should be he proposed working through a famous treatise on fugue by Friedrich Wilhelm Marpurg (1718–95), with the help of a fine teacher. On November 12 he was in bed and four days later it was clear that he had not long to live. Typhoid fever was diagnosed; but Schubert's body, racked with infection, was a mass of disease. He died on November 19, and two days later was buried in the same cemetery as Beethoven.

10. *Posthumous Fame*

SCHUBERT NOW RANKS among the dozen or so great musicians of all time, of whom few are as familiar or popular. The reason for this lies on the one hand in his supreme mastery of his medium, on the other in the way in which he used this to represent not only his own hopes, fears, and aspirations, doubts, and discontents, but those of all, at all times, who wish to see a better world.

A week, a year, or a decade after his death few people, even in Vienna, cared about the reputation of Franz Schubert. Many of his works remained unpublished, unperformed, and unknown.

When he was a student Robert Schumann took great pleasure in Schubert's music. So much so that in the last year of Schubert's life he wrote a letter to him to say so. Unfortunately, and characteristically, he forgot to send this letter. He continued, however, to study Schubert's music eagerly, and in 1838 he visited Ferdinand Schubert in Vienna from whom he obtained the score of the C major Symphony.

Schumann showed this work to Felix Mendelssohn, who, sharing his enthusiasm, arranged to perform it with the Leipzig Gewandhaus Orchestra. The first performance took place on March 21, 1839. This was almost ten years to the day after Mendelssohn had given the first performance of Bach's *St Matthew Passion* since that composer's death.

Despite Schumann's campaigning as music critic, and Mendelssohn's advocacy as conductor, the idea that Schubert was one of the great masters was a long time in taking hold.

In 1844 Mendelssohn took the score of the C major Symphony—which had by now been published—to England. The members of the Philharmonic Society orchestra laughed at the music and said that they were not going to play such stuff. But the German-born conductor of the orchestra established at the Crystal Palace, London, in 1856, August Manns, was a keen Schubertian and insisted on including the C major Symphony in his concerts. Ten years later George Grove, Secretary of the Crystal Palace and a friend of Manns, wrote to Vienna asking that whatever of Schubert was newly published should be sent to him for inclusion in the Crystal Palace programmes.

A year later Grove travelled to Vienna in the hope of finding more works by Schubert that had never seen the light of day. He took with him a young composer, Arthur Sullivan, who for his part had developed his appreciation of Schubert when a student in Leipzig. Grove and Sullivan talked with Joseph Doppler, manager of one of the music houses that had published Schubert's works, with Eduard Schneider, Schubert's nephew, and with the officials of the Society for Friends of Music. In the end, after turning up various scores and sets of parts of music by Schubert, they found what they had really set out to find. This was the complete music for the play *Rosamunde*. On November 10 this was played for the first time at the Crystal Palace, in London, with Manns conducting.

While the greater works of Schubert were thus being introduced into the concert repertoire the songs were becoming not only popular but an indispensable part of the general experience of music. In days when knowledge of music depended largely on the ability of the amateur to make his own music Schubert's songs opened new vistas. Some six hundred songs—each with its own measure of individuality —give that number of impressions of human existence in all its phases.

It is small wonder that Schumann could write:

The work he has left behind him is to us a cherished bequest; time may yet produce countless and noble things, but never again a Schubert.

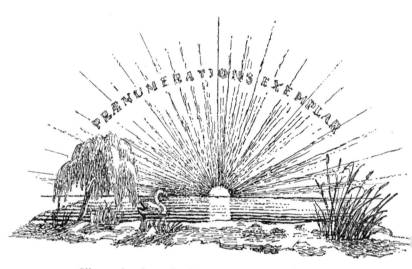

Illustration from the first edition of Schwanengesang

Index

References to illustrations are shown in italic type

Printed in Great Britain by The Bowering Press, Plymouth